the promise of Joy

Kathy Wagoner

SOURCEBOOKS, INC.
NAPERVILLE, ILLINOIS

Published by Sourcebooks, Inc.
P.O. Box 4410, Naperville, Illinois 60567-4410
(630) 961-3900
FAX: (630) 961-2168
www.sourcebooks.com
ISBN 1-4022-0023-4

Printed and bound in the United States of America
IN 10 9 8 7 6 5 4 3 2 1

On with the dance!

Let joy be unconfined.

—George Gordon, Lord Byron

Write it on your heart

that every day is the best

day in the year.

—Ralph Waldo Emerson

JOY

A kind heart
is a fountain of gladness,
making everything
in its vicinity freshen
into smiles.

—Washington Irving

One of the secrets of a long and fruitful life is to forgive everyone everything every night before you go to bed.

—Ann Landers

Liberty, like day,
Breaks on the
soul, and by
a flash from
Heav'n Fires all
the faculties with
glorious joy.

—William Cowper

Every joy is gain
And gain is gain,
however small.
—Robert Browning

Give one health and a *course to steer*, and you'll never stop to trouble about whether you're *happy* or not.

—George Bernard Shaw

How true it is that what we really see day by day depends less on the objects and scenes before our eyes than on the eyes themselves and the minds and hearts that use them.

—F.D. Huntington

The better part of **happiness** is to wish to be what you are.

—Desiderius Erasmus

Make *happy* those
who are near, and
those who are far
will come.

—Chinese proverb

I never admired
another's
fortune so
much that
I became
dissatisfied
with my own.

—Cicero

Happiness is essentially
a state of going somewhere,
wholeheartedly, one-directionally,
without regret or reservation.

—William H. Sheldon

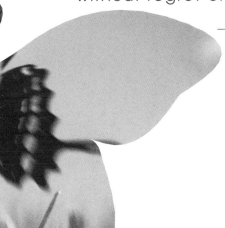

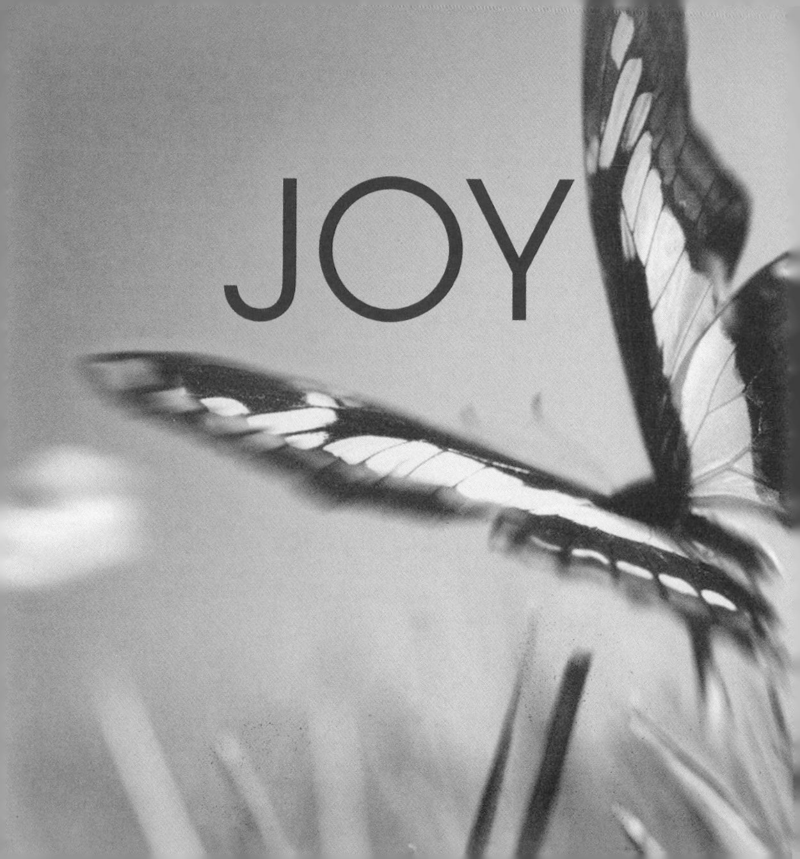
JOY

Challenges make you

discover things about

yourself that you

never really knew.

—Cicely Tyson

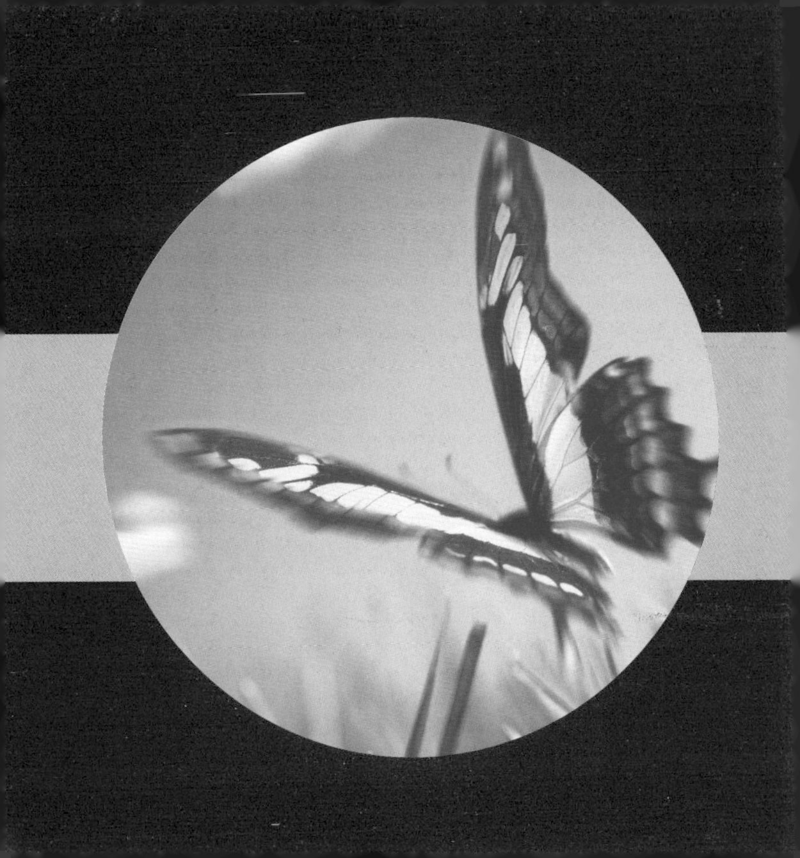

The ancient Greek definition of happiness was the full use of your powers along lines of excellence.

—John F. Kennedy

After every storm
the sun will smile;
for every problem
there is a solution,
and the soul's
indefeasible duty is
to be of good cheer.

—William R. Alger

Shared joy is
double joy.
Shared sorrow is
half a sorrow.

—Swedish proverb

All events are
linked up in this
the best of all
possible worlds.

—Voltaire

If life were predictable, it would cease to be life and would be without flavor.

—Eleanor Roosevelt

When spring is dancing among the hills, one should not stay in a little dark corner.

—Kahlil Gibran

My bosom underwent a glorious glow, and my internal spirit cut a caper.

—George Gordon, Lord Byron

There is a miracle in

every new beginning.

—Herman Hesse

JOY

Love comforteth
like *sunshine* after rain.

—William Shakespeare

"Hope" is the thing with feathers—That perches in the soul—And sings the tune without the words—
And never stops—at all.

—Emily Dickinson

To love and be
loved is to feel
the sun from
both sides.

—David Viscott

Happiness makes up
in height for what it
lacks in length.

—Robert Frost

You can't prevent birds of sorrow from flying over your head, but you *can prevent* them from building nests in your hair.

—Chinese proverb

One must not lose
desires. They are
mighty stimulants to
creativeness, to love,
and to long life.

—Alexander A. Bogomoletz

We must always have
old memories, and
young hopes.

—Arsene Houssaye

Life is no brief candle to me; it is a
sort of splendid torch which I have
got hold of for the moment, and
I want to make it burn as brightly as
possible before handing it on to
future generations.

—George Bernard Shaw

The best way

to cheer yourself

up is to try to

cheer someone

else up.

—Mark Twain

When large numbers of
people share their joy in
common, the happiness
of each is greater
because
each
adds fuel
to the other's
flame.

—Saint Augustine

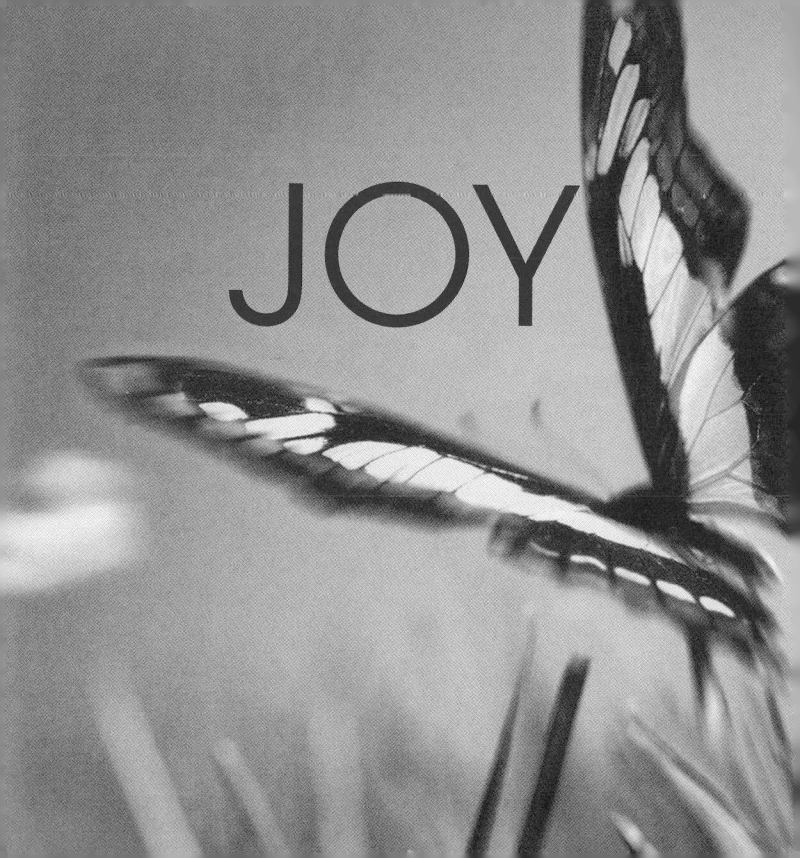
JOY

Happiness is not something you get, but something you do.

—Marcelene Cox

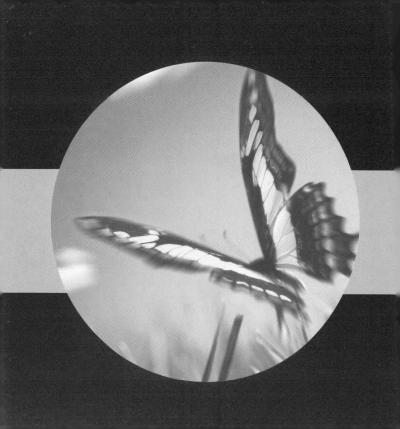

There is no medicine like hope,
no incentive so great, and no
tonic so powerful as expectation
of something tomorrow.

—O.S. Marden

Happiness is found along the way—not at the end of the road.

—Sol Gordon

There is very little difference in people, but that little difference makes a big difference. The little difference is attitude. The big difference is whether it is positive or negative.

—Clement Stone

Self-trust is the first secret of success.

—Ralph Waldo Emerson

Some things
have to be
believed to
be seen.

—Ralph Hodgson

Far away there in the sunshine are my highest aspirations. I may not reach them, but I can look up and see their beauty, believe in them, and try to follow where they lead.

—Louisa May Alcott

The moments when you have really lived are the moments when you have done things in the spirit of love.

—Henry Drummond

He who binds
to himself a joy

Does the winged
life destroy;

But he who kisses
the joy as it flies

Lives in eternity's sunrise.

—William Blake

JOY

Just to be is a blessing.
Just to live is holy.

—Abraham Heschel

Love demands that I learn

how to focus my attention

on the needs of those I love.

—John Powell

The hopeful man
sees success
where others see
failure, sunshine
where others
see shadows
and storm.

—O.S. Marden

I am not concerned that you have fallen; I am concerned that you arise.

—Abraham Lincoln

True ecstasy hails neither
from spirit nor from
nature, but from the
union of these two.

—Martin Buber

Experience is not what happens to *you*. It is what *you do* with what happens to *you*.

—Aldous Huxley

Happiness is as a butterfly, which, when pursued, is always beyond our grasp, but which, if you will sit down quietly, may alight upon you.

—Nathaniel Hawthorne

Regret is an appalling waste of energy, you can't build on it; it's only good for wallowing in.

—Katherine Mansfield

No matter what part of the world we come from, we are all basically the same human beings. We all seek happiness and try to avoid suffering.

—His Holiness, the Dalai Lama

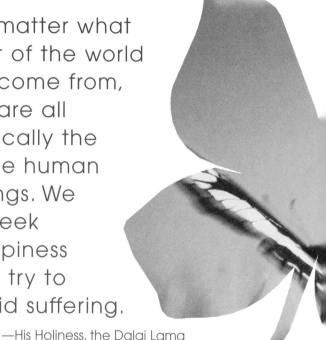

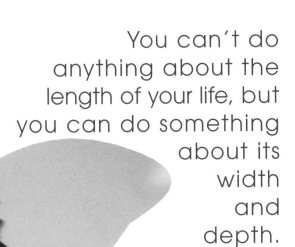

You can't do anything about the length of your life, but you can do something about its width and depth.

—Evan Esar

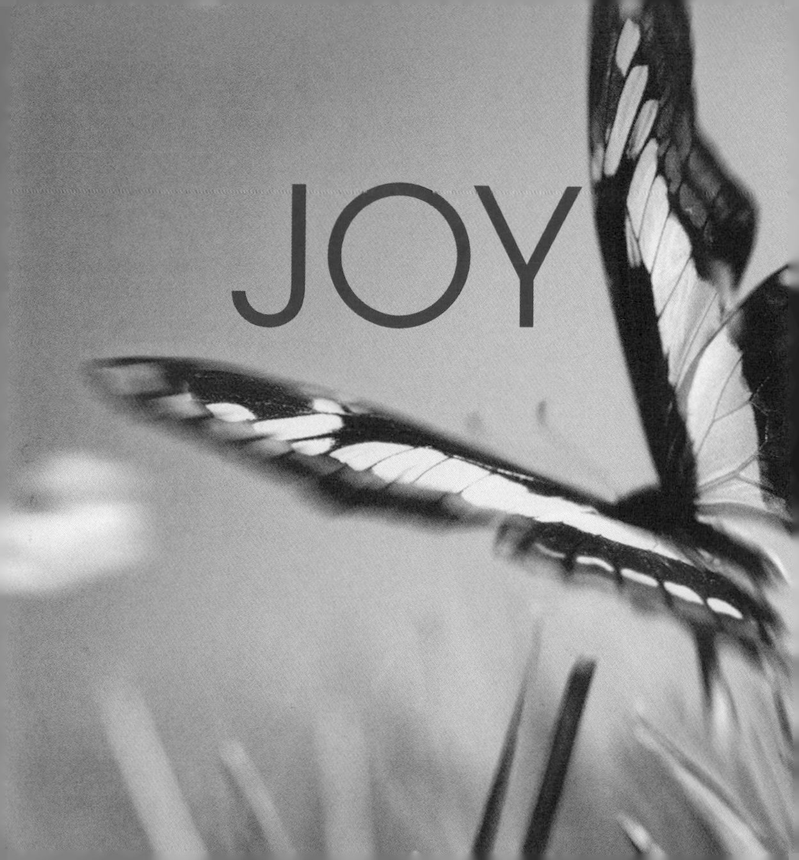
JOY

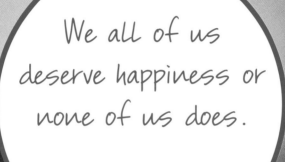

We all of us
deserve happiness or
none of us does.

—Mary Gordon

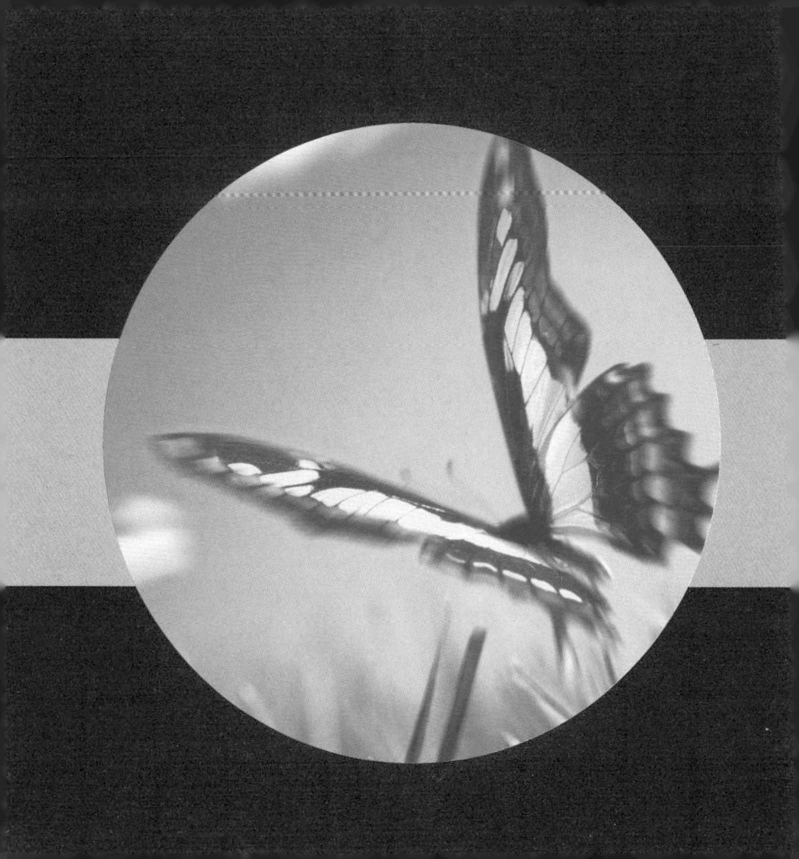

Life is a glass given
to us to fill.

—William Brown

Happiness is a habit—cultivate it.

—Elbert Hubbard

The grand essentials

in this life are something

to do, something

to love, and something

to hope for.

—Joseph Addison

Life can only
be understood
backwards; but
it must be lived
forwards.

—Søren Kierkegaard

Blessed are
they who know
how to shine
on one's
gloom with
their cheer.

—Henry Ward Beecher

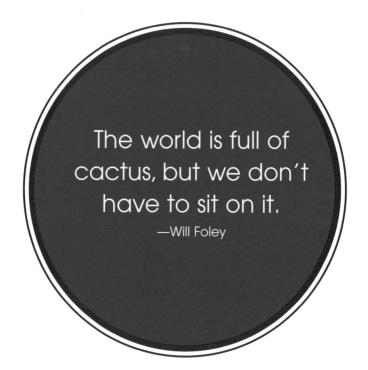

The world is full of
cactus, but we don't
have to sit on it.

—Will Foley

Be sure to live on
the *sunny side,*
and even then do not
expect the world
to look bright if
you habitually wear
gray-brown glasses.

—Charles Eliot

There never shall be one lost good. All we have willed or hoped or dreamed of good shall exist.

—Robert Browning

JOY

A man's life is dyed the color of his imagination.

—Marcus Aurelius

What the heart has

once owned and had,

it shall never lose.

—Henry Ward Beecher

The sky is the

daily bread of

the eyes.

—Ralph Waldo Emerson

The world is not conclusion;
A sequel stands beyond...

—Emily Dickinson

Life is too short
to be small.

—Benjamin Disraeli

Most folks are about

as happy as they make

up their minds to be.

—Abraham Lincoln

Happiness comes of the capacity to feel deeply, to enjoy simply, to think freely, to risk life, to be needed!
—Storm Jameson

Let us be of good cheer,
however, remembering that
the misfortunes hardest
to bear are those
which never come.

—James Russell Lowell

As a tale, so is life:
not how long it is,
but *how good* it is,
is what matters.

—Seneca

People *need joy* quite as much as clothing. Some of them need it far more.

—Margaret Collier Graham

JOY

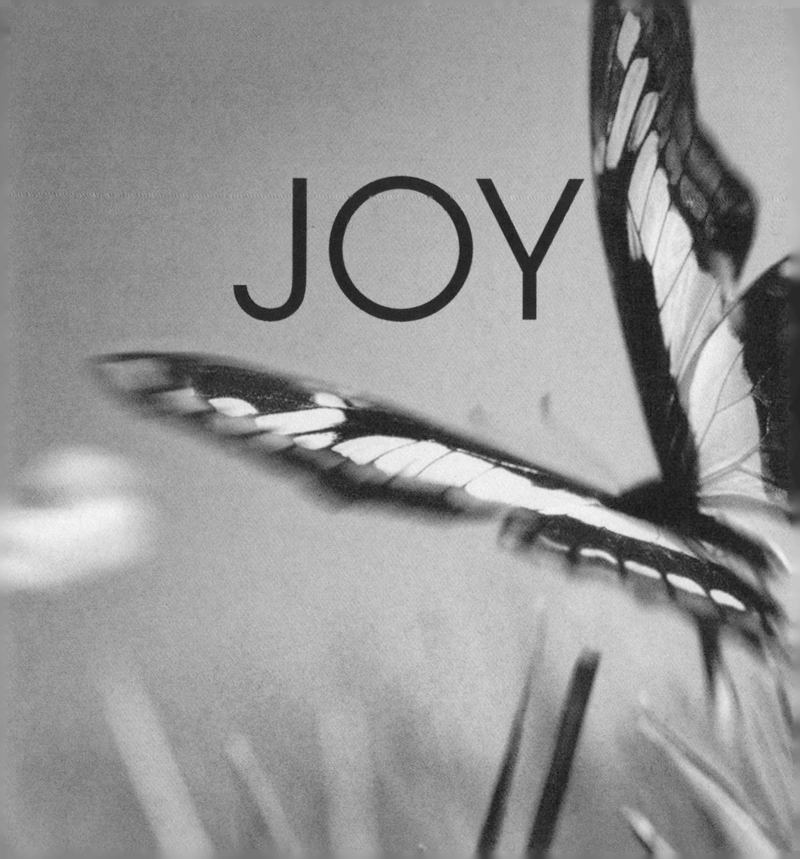

Blessed is he who has

learned to laugh at himself,

for he shall never cease

to be entertained.

—John Bowell

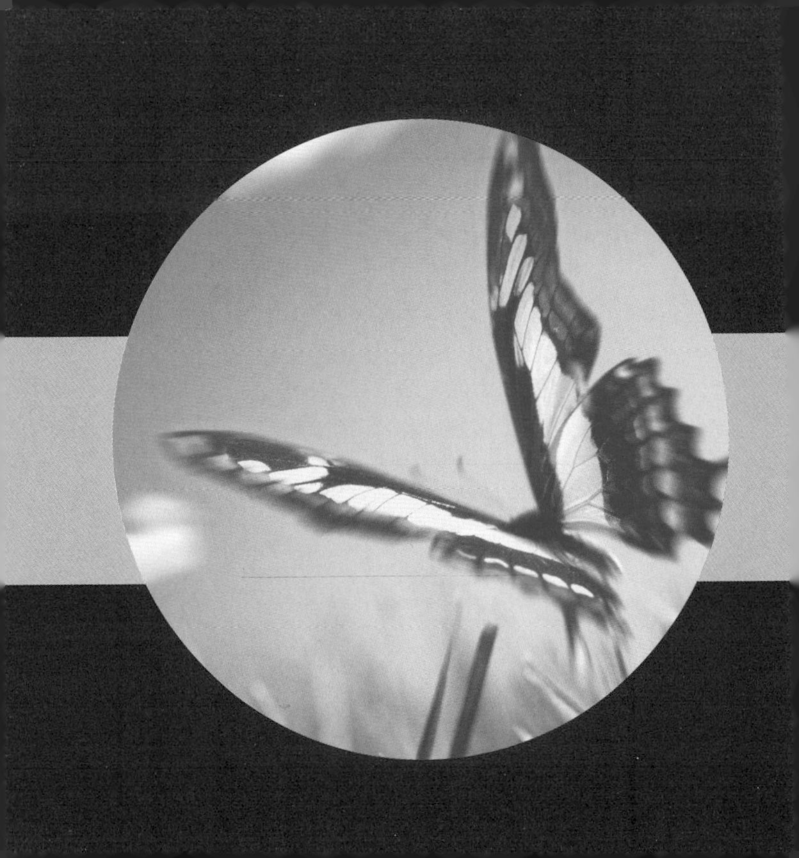

Courage—an independent spark
from heaven's bright throne,
by which the soul stands raised
triumphant, high, alone.
—George Farquhar

A sure way to lose happiness,
I found, is to want it at the
expense of everything else.

—Bette Davis

Daylight will peep
through a very
small hole.

—Japanese proverb

You give but
little when you
give of your
possessions. It is
when you give
of yourself that
you truly give.

—Kahlil Gibran

Every human
being is intended
to have a
character of his
own; to be what
no other is, and
to do what no
other can do.

—William Channing

Surely the strange
beauty of the world
must somewhere
rest on pure joy!

—Louise Bogan

All the wonders you

seek are within yourself.

—Sir Thomas Brown

One of the loveliest remarks that one person can make regarding another is that which was made by Nathaniel Hawthorne of his wife. Said he, "I never knew what spiritual refreshment meant until I met her."

—Douglas Horton

JOY

A single sunbeam is
enough to drive away
many shadows.

—Saint Francis of Assisi

There is always hope for an individual who stops to do some serious thinking about life.

—Katherine Logan

A thing of beauty

is a joy forever:

Its loveliness

increases; it will

never pass into

nothingness.

—John Keats

I never met a man
I didn't like.

—Will Rogers

In the time of your

life—*Live!*

—William Saroyan

Silence is the perfectest herald of joy: I were but little happy, if I could say how much.

—William Shakespeare

My heart leaps up
when I behold a
rainbow in the sky.

—William Wordsworth

Everyone has, inside himself...what shall I call it? *A piece of good news!* Everyone is...a very great, very important character!

—Ugo Betti

When you make
a world tolerable
for *yourself*,
you make a
world tolerable
for *others*.

—Anaïs Nin

Good communication is stimulating as black coffee, and just as hard to sleep after.

—Anne Morrow Lindbergh

JOY

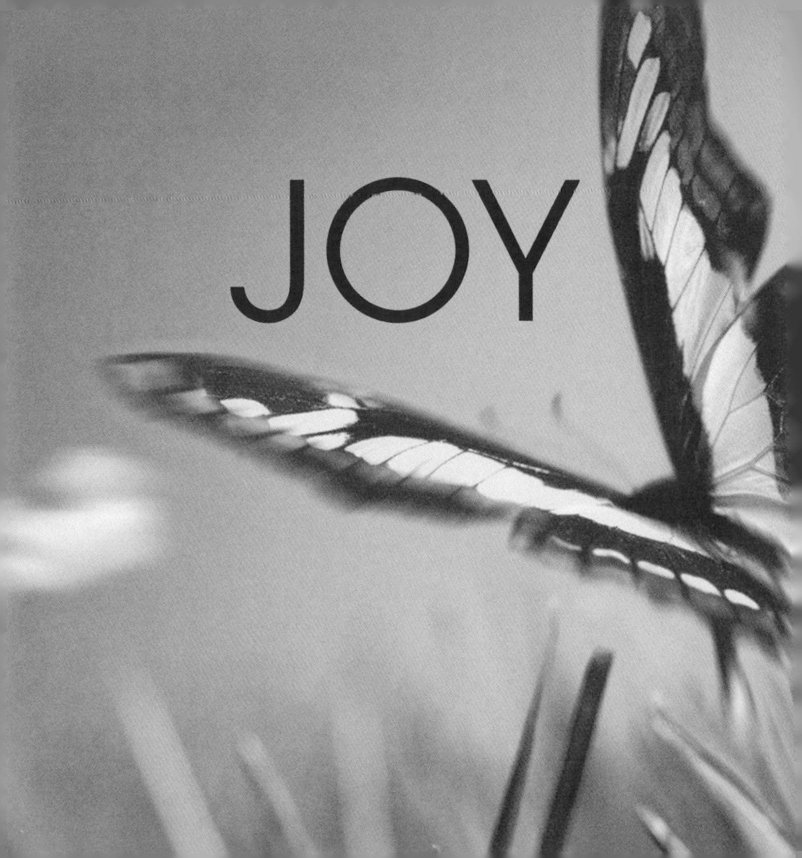

Happiness lies
in the consciousness
we have of it.

—George Sand

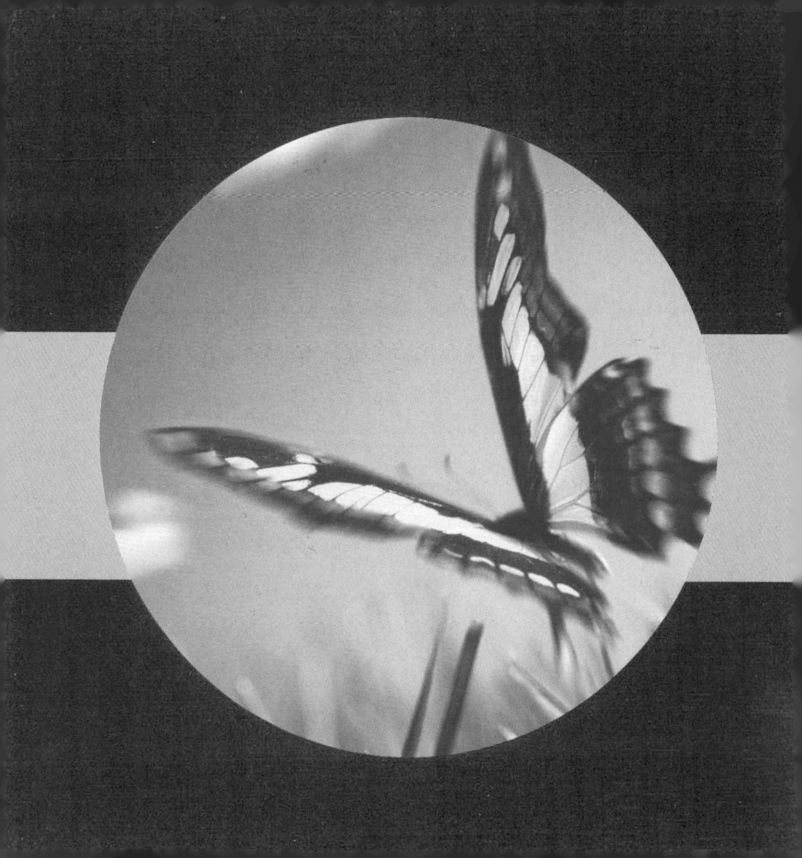

The future belongs to
those who believe in the
beauty of their dreams.

—Eleanor Roosevelt

He has achieved success
who has lived well, laughed
often, and loved much.

—Mrs. A.J. Stanley

106

Getting what you go

after is success; but

liking it while you are

getting it is happiness.

—Bertha Damon

Weep if thou
wilt, but weep
not all too long;
Or weep and
work, for work
will lead
to song.

—George MacDonald

Variety
is the soul of
pleasure.

—Aphra Behn

Things are only worth what one makes them worth.

—Moliere

Adventure

is worthwhile in itself.

—Amelia Earhart

It is never too late
to be what you
might have been.

—George Eliot

JOY

Tomorrow to fresh woods,
and pastures new.

—John Milton

All things change,

nothing perishes.

—Ovid

Fortify
yourself with
contentment,
for this is an
impregnable
fortress.

—Epictetus

Have you had a kindness
shown? Pass it on.

—Henry Burton

A thing is important if

anyone think it important.

—William James

Your life will be
rich for others only
as it is rich for you.

—David McCord

Happiness itself is a
kind of gratitude.

—Joseph Wood Krutch

When one door
closes, fortune will
usually open another.

—Fernando de Rojas

It is my personal approach that creates the climate. It is my *daily mood* that makes the weather.

—Haim Ginott

When one door of happiness
closes, another opens; but
often we look so long at the
closed door
that we
do not
see the one
which has been
opened for us.

—Helen Keller

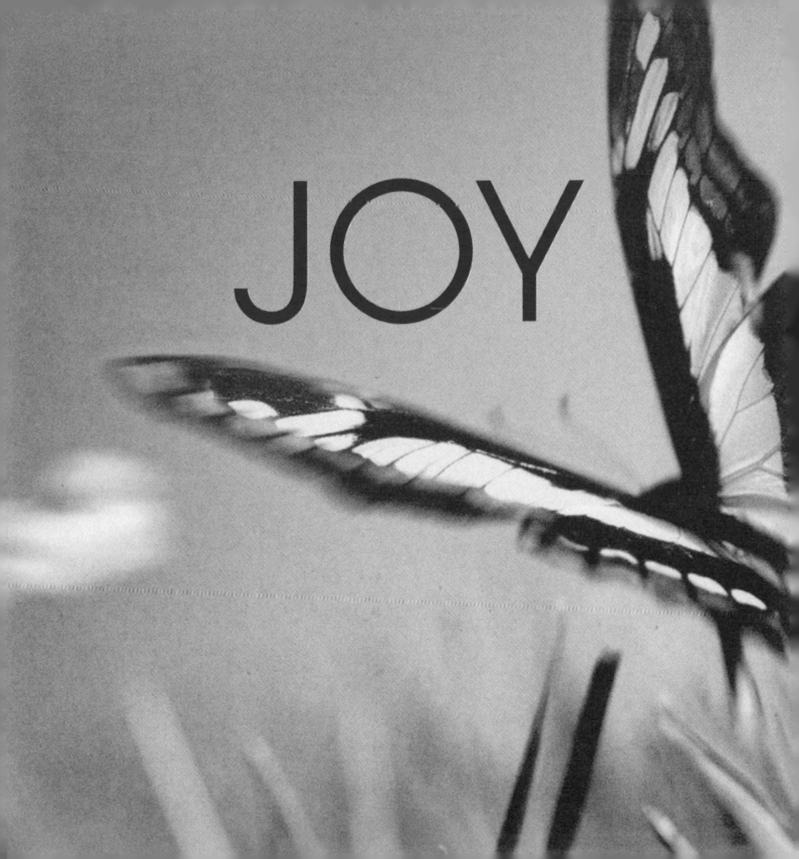
JOY

Tomorrow
will be a new day.

—Miguel de Cervantes

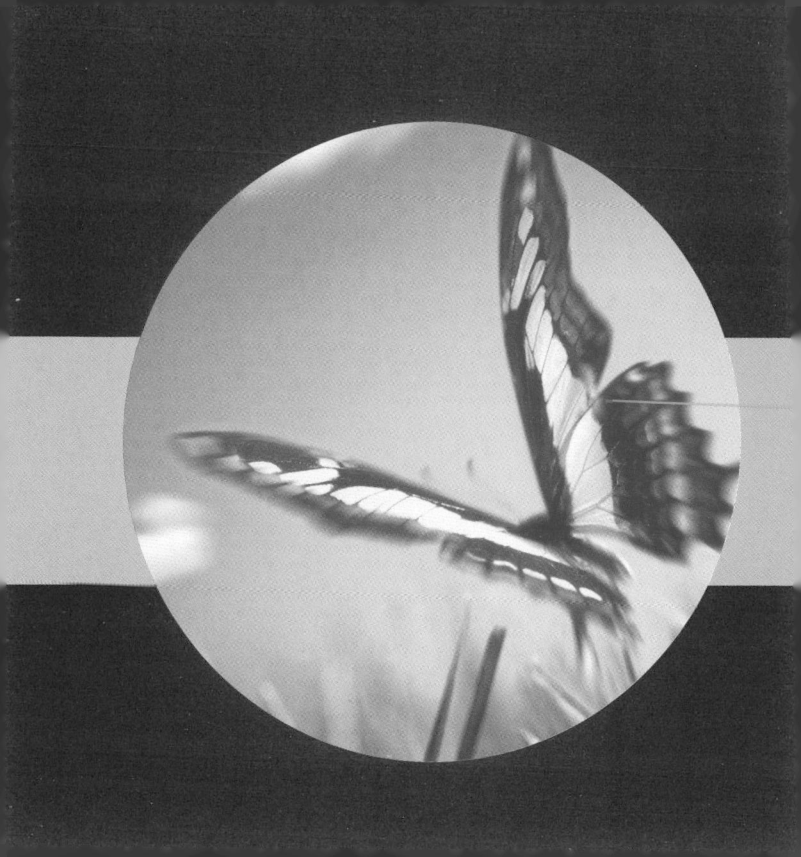

What wisdom can
you find that is greater
than kindness?

—Jean Jacques Rousseau

We know nothing of tomorrow;
our business is to be good
and happy today.

—Sydney Smith

128

Happiness is at once
the best, the noblest,
and the pleasantest
of things.

—Aristotle

The hope of
life returns
with the sun.

—Decimus Junius Juvenal

The foolish
man seeks
happiness in the
distance;
the wise grows it
under his feet.

—James Oppenheim

At times the sight of
a mountain of felicity
will not raise a man's spirits;
at other times, if his foot trips
over a molehill, he will
cry out in ecstasy at the
goodness of life.
—John Boynton Priestley

Happiness is not
a matter of events; it
depends upon the
tides of the mind.

—Alice Meynell

Vigorous health and its

accompanying high spirits are

larger elements of happiness

than any other things whatever.

—Herbert Spencer

JOY

The essence of pleasure
is *spontaneity*.

—Germaine Greer

Let us be grateful to people who make us happy; they are the charming gardeners who make our souls blossom.

—Marcel Proust

Uncertainty
and expectation
are the joys
of life.

—Richard Congreve

Every day stop before something beautiful long enough to say, "Isn't that b-e-a-u-t-i-f-u-l."
—Alice Freeman Palmer

One cannot have

pleasure without *giving it.*

—Hermann Hesse

Gratitude
is the memory
of the heart.

—Jean Baptiste Massieu

Hope is a waking
dream.

—Aristotle

Every life is a
profession of faith,
and exercises an
inevitable and
silent influence.

—Henri-Frederic Amiel

That is *happiness*:
to be dissolved
into something
complete
and *great*.

—Willa Cather

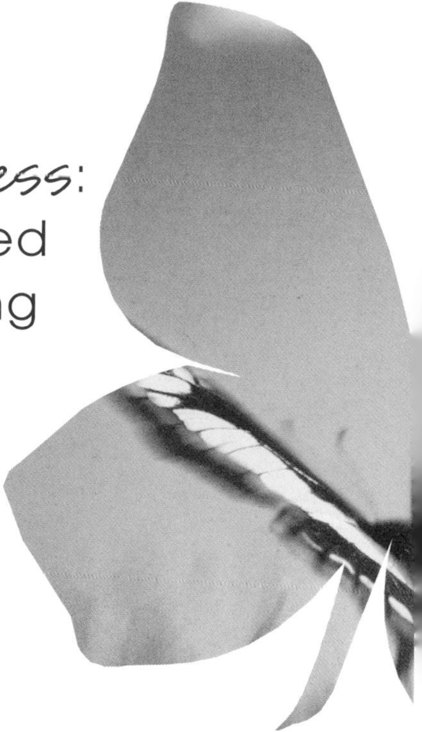

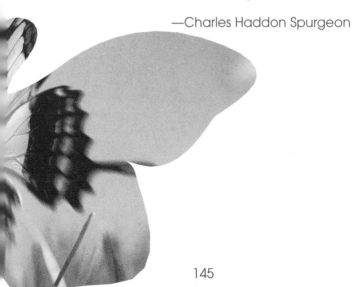

There is a sweet joy
which comes to us
through sorrow.

—Charles Haddon Spurgeon

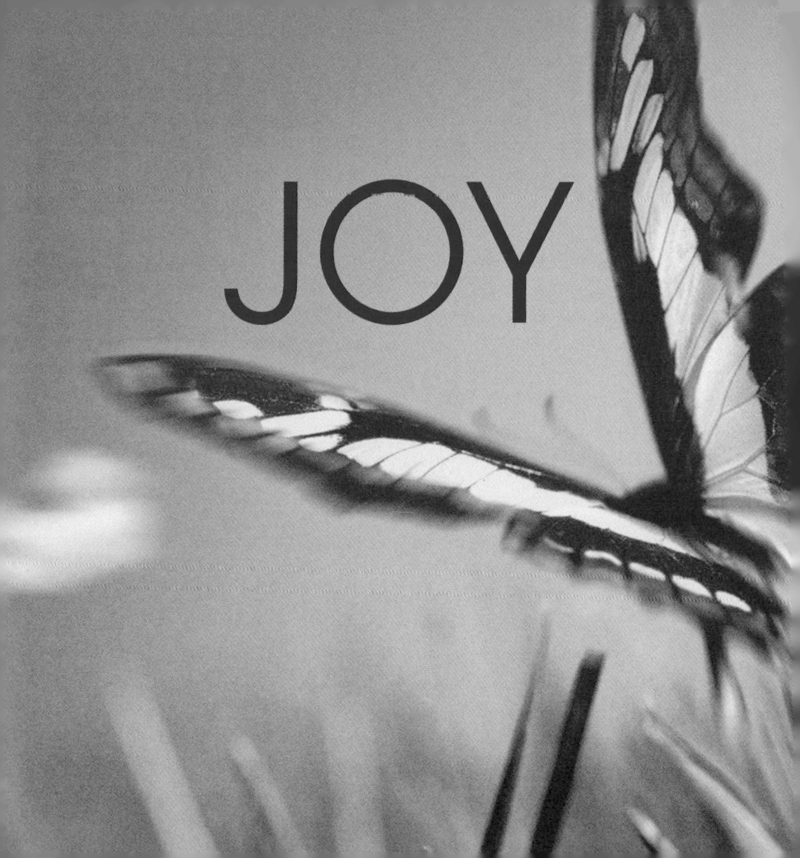
JOY

Miracles are to those

who believe in them.

—W. Gurney Benham

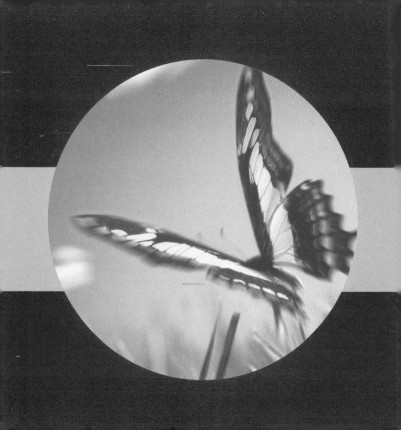

Life is a pure flame, and we live by an invisible sun within us.

—Sir Thomas Browne

In seed time learn,
in harvest teach, in
winter *enjoy*.

—William Blake

Life may take away happiness. But it can't take away having had it.

—Ellen Glasgow

Happiness is
not a station
you arrive at,
but a manner
of traveling.

—Margaret Lee Runbeck

Choose the best life; habit will make it pleasant.

—Epictetus

That which is bitter to endure may be sweet to remember.

—Thomas Fuller

Life is short,

and we have never too
much time for gladdening the
hearts of those who are travelling
the dark journey with us. Oh,
be swift to love, make
haste to be kind.

—Henri-Frederic Amiel

'Tis always morning

somewhere in the world.

—Richard Hengest Horne

JOY

Mirth prolongeth life,
and causeth health.

—Nicholas Udall

To all upon my way,

Day after day,

Let me be joy, be hope.

Let my life sing!

—Mary Carolyn Davies

To look up
and not down,
To look forward
and not back,
To look out
and not in
And to lend
a hand.

—Edward Everett Hale

Every thing that grows
Holds in perfection but a
little moment.

—William Shakespeare

The days that make us

happy make us wise.

—John Masefield

Work is love made visible.
If you bake bread with
indifference, you bake a
bitter bread that feeds
but half a man's hunger.

—Kahlil Gibran

Happiness sneaks
in through a door
you didn't know
you left open.

—John Barrymore

Even if we can't be happy, we must always be cheerful.

—Irving Kristol

We are living in a
new era in the land
of beginning again.
The boundary of
your dreams is
the measure of
your success.
Dare to dream.

—Elma Easley

Variety is
the soul
of pleasure.

—Aphra Behn

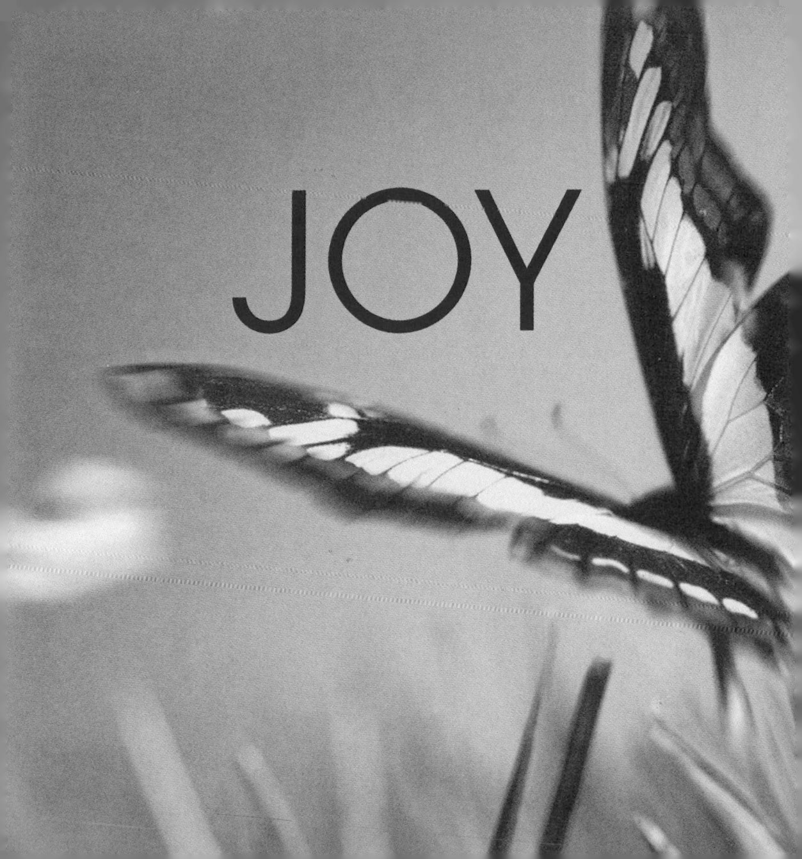
JOY

The best part of health

is fine disposition.

—Ralph Waldo Emerson

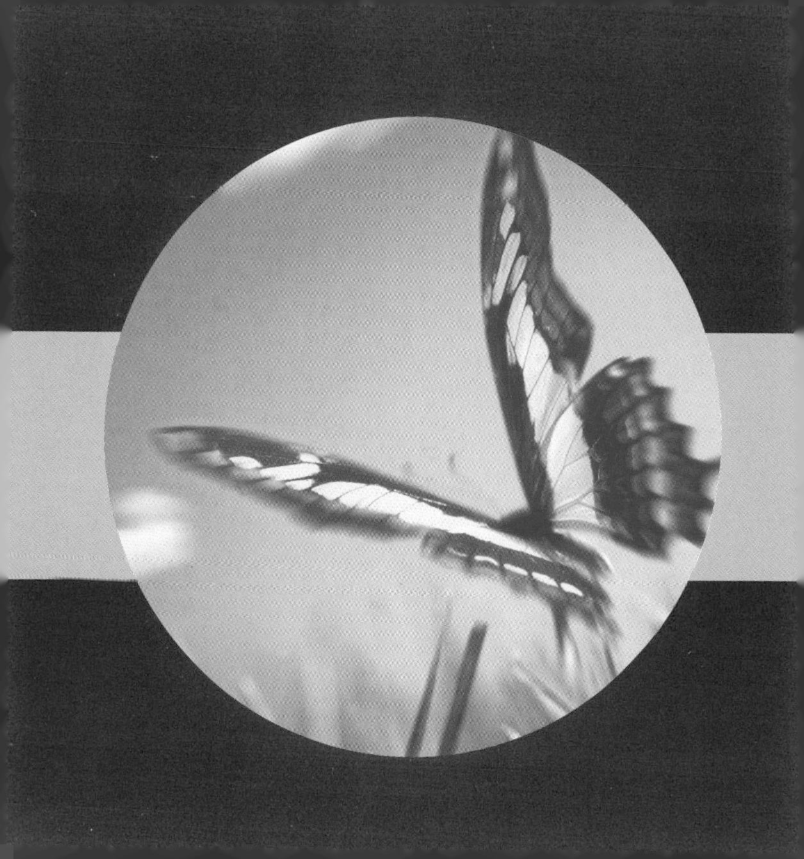

No duty is more
urgent than that of
returning thanks.

—Saint Ambrose

Cheerfulness, it would
appear, is a matter which
depends fully as much on
the state of things within, as
on the state of things
without and around us.

—Charlotte Brontë

Happiness

depends upon

ourselves.

—Aristotle

Joy is not
in things;
it is in us.

—Richard Wagner

Whoever is
happy will
make others
happy too.

—Anne Frank

It is in his pleasure that a man really lives; it is from his leisure that he constructs the true fabric of self.

Agnes Repplier

We find a delight in the beauty and happiness of children, that makes the heart too big for the body.

—Ralph Waldo Emerson

Adventures are to the

adventurous.

—Benjamin Disraeli

JOY

If you have much,
give of your wealth;
if you have little,
give of your heart.

—Arab proverb

One who knows how to

show and to accept

kindness will be a friend

better than any possession.

—Sophocles

Never lose

a chance

of saying a

kind word.

—William Makepeace
Thackeray

I am seeking, I am striving,
I am in it with all my heart.

—Vincent van Gogh

In things pertaining to
enthusiasm, no man is
sane who does not
know how to be insane
on proper occasions.

—Henry Ward Beecher

Goodness is easier
to recognize than
to define.

—W.H. Auden

Never bend your head.
Always hold it high.
Look the world
straight in the eye.

—Helen Keller

In spite of everything,
I still believe that
people are really
good at heart.

—Anne Frank

I long to accomplish a great and noble task, but it is my chief duty to accomplish small tasks as if they were great and noble.

—Helen Keller

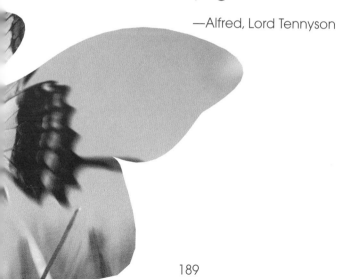

Love is the
only gold.

—Alfred, Lord Tennyson

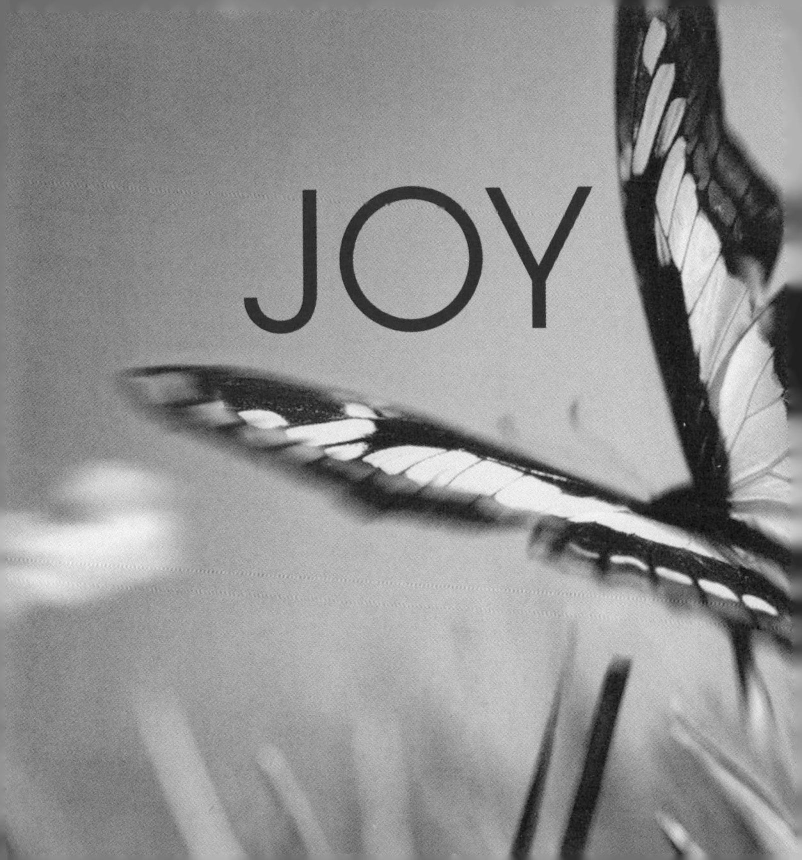

JOY

The supreme happiness
of life is the conviction
that we are loved; loved
for ourselves—say rather,
loved in spite of ourselves.

—Victor Hugo

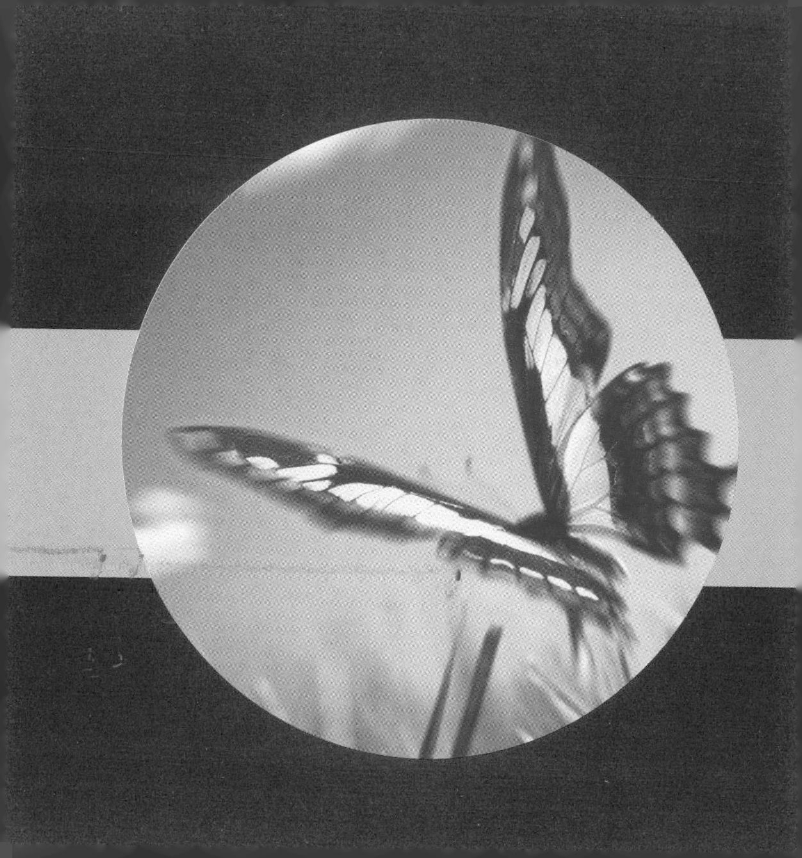

Love is a
beautiful dream.

—William Sharp

The *only gift* is a
portion of thyself.

—Ralph Waldo Emerson

194

The happiness of life is made of minute fractions—the little, soon forgotten charities of a kiss or smile, a kind look, a heartfelt compliment, and the countless infinitesimals of pleasurable and genial feeling.

—Samuel Taylor Coleridge

A mind always
employed is
always happy.
This is the true
secret, the
grand recipe,
for felicity.

—Thomas Jefferson

My message to you is this: Be courageous. Have faith. Go forward!

—Thomas Edison

Happy the man,

and happy he alone,

He who can call today his own;

He who, secure within, can say,

Tomorrow, do thy worst,

for I have liv'd today.

—John Dryden

If the day and night be such that you greet them with joy, and life emits a fragrance like flowers and sweet-scented herbs, is more elastic, more immortal—that is your success. All nature is your congratulation, and you have cause momentarily to bless yourself.

—Henry David Thoreau

Be like the bird

That, pausing in her flight

Awhile on boughs too slight,

Feels them give way

Beneath her and yet sings,

Knowing that she hath wings.

—Victor Hugo

JOY

The gloom of the world
is but a shadow; behind
it, yet within our reach,
is joy. Take joy.

—Fra Giovanni

The true harvest of my daily life

is somewhat as intangible and

indescribable as the tints of

morning or evening. It is a little

stardust caught, a segment of

the rainbow which I have clutched.

—Henry David Thoreau

Happiness consists more in small conveniences or pleasures that occur every day, than in great pieces of good fortune that happen but seldom.

—Benjamin Franklin

Never run out of goals.

—Earl Nightingale

Happiness

is contagious.

—Hubert H. Humphrey

Opportunity is limitless.
Where there is an open
mind, there will always
be a frontier.

—Charles F. Kettering

A person can do
other things against
his will; but belief is
possible only in one
who is willing.

—Saint Augustine

All the kindness which
a man puts out into
the world works on
the heart and
thoughts of mankind.

—Albert Schweitzer

There may be
Peace without Joy,
and Joy without
Peace, but the two
combined make
happiness.

—John Buchan

To bring joy to a single heart is better than to build many shrines for worship.

—Abu Sa'id Ibn Abi Khayr

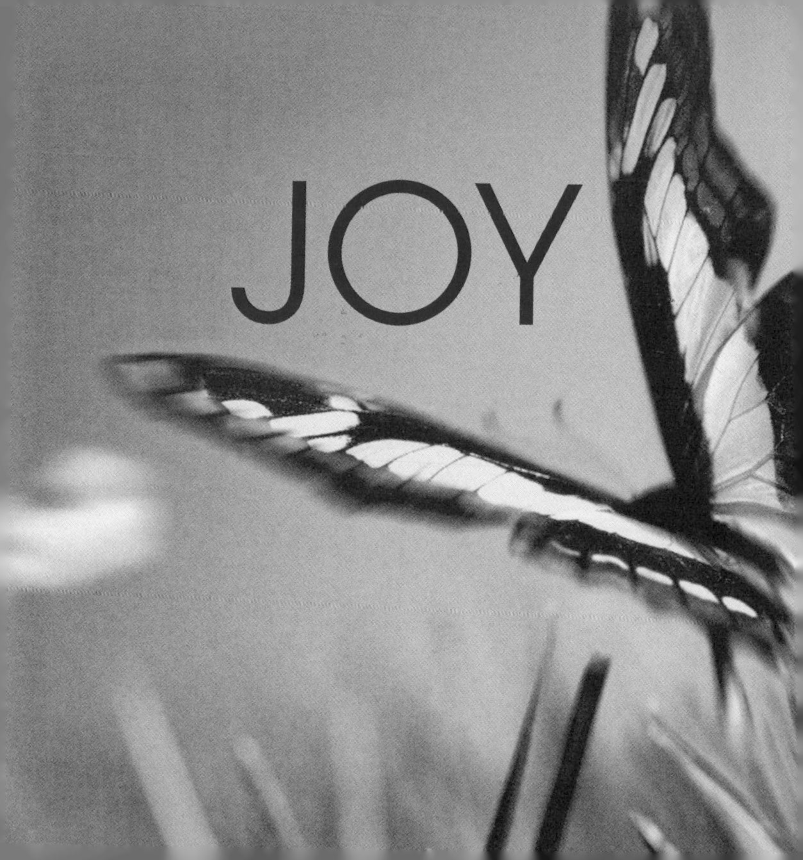
JOY

The joy of a good man is the witness of a good conscience; have a good conscience and thou shalt ever have gladness.

—Thomas á Kempis

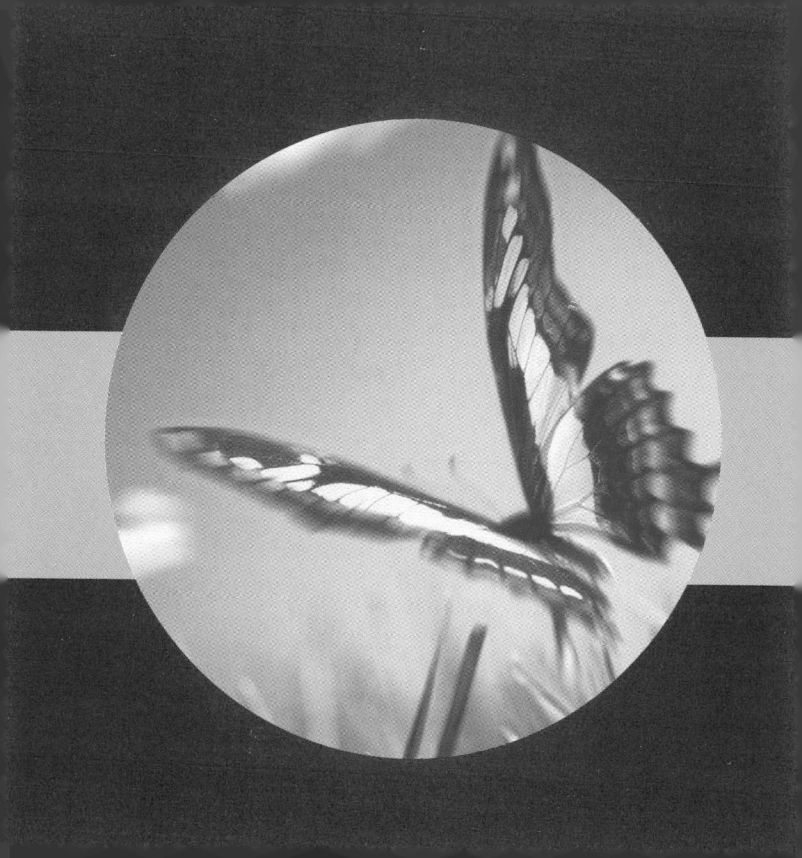

All that we are is
the result of what
we have thought.

—Dhammapada

Shall we make a new rule of life...Always to try to be a little kinder than is necessary?

—James M. Barrie

It is neither
wealth nor splendor,
but *tranquillity* and
occupation which
give *happiness*.

—Thomas Jefferson

There is more
to life than
increasing
its speed.

—Mohandas K. Gandhi

Life becomes
harder for us
when we live
for others, but it
also becomes
richer and
happier.

—Albert Schweitzer

The most astonishing thing about miracles is that they happen.

—G.K. Chesterton

Happiness is not a possession to be prized, it is a quality of thought, a state of mind.

—Daphne du Maurier

Happiness always looks
small while you hold
it in your hands, but
let it go, and you learn
at once how big
and *precious it is.*

—Maxim Gorky

JOY

Happiness is the meaning
and the purpose of life,
the whole aim and end
of human existence.

—Aristotle

The pursuit of happiness...is the greatest feat man has to accomplish.

—Robert Henri

This is life!
It can harden
and it can exalt!

—Henrik Ibsen

Happiness…leads none of us by the same route.

—Charles Caleb Colton

Instinct teaches us to

look for happiness

outside ourselves.

—Blaise Pascal

Learn
how
to
feel
joy.

—Seneca

To do the useful thing, to say the courageous thing, to contemplate the beautiful thing: that is enough for one man's life.

—T.S. Eliot

Simplicity, clarity, singleness: these are the attributes that give our lives power and vividness and joy.

—Richard Halloway

Everyone, without exception, is searching for happiness.

—Blaise Pascal

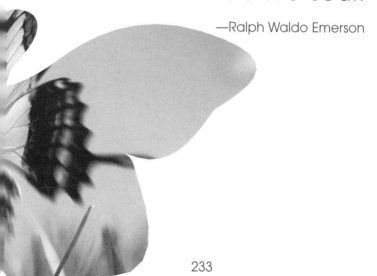

The one thing in
the world, of value,
is the active soul.

—Ralph Waldo Emerson

JOY

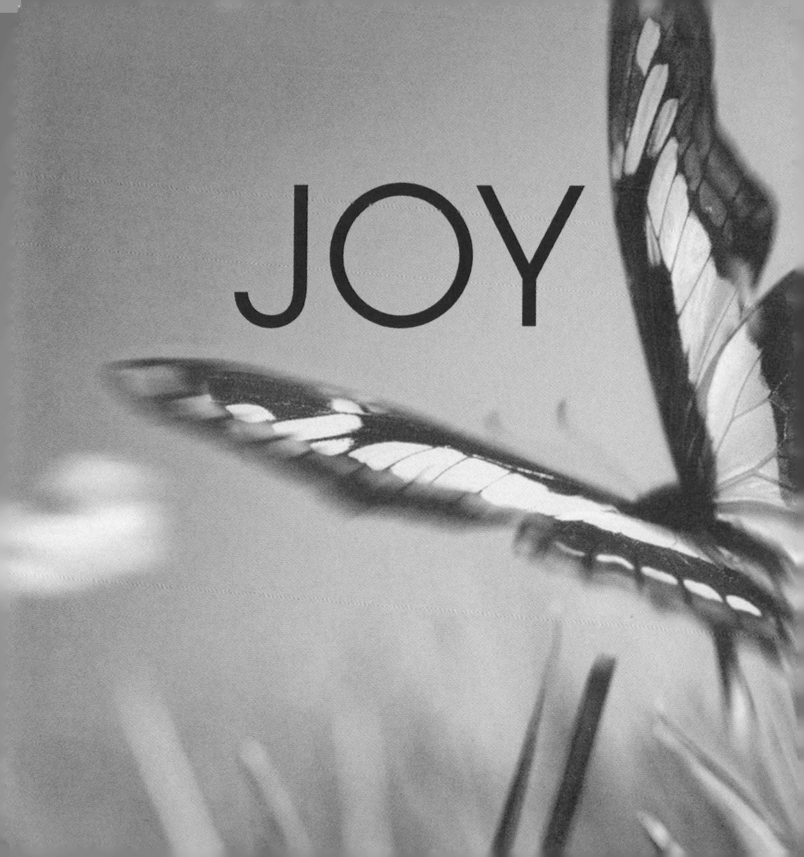

Wherever there is a human being there is an opportunity for a kindness.

—Seneca

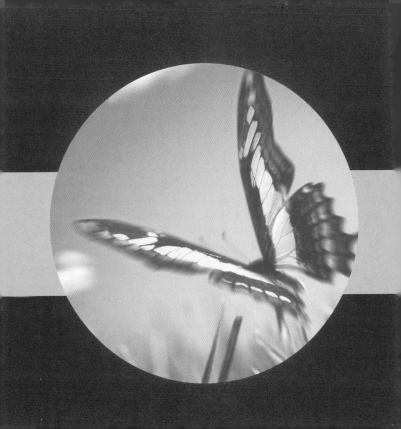

There's a time
for all things.

—William Shakespeare

Happy is the one who forgets that which cannot be changed.

—German proverb

Kindness gives

birth to kindness.

—Sophocles

Although
the world is
very full of
suffering, it is
also full of the
overcoming
of it.

—Helen Keller

The Wright
brothers flew
right through
the smoke
screen of
impossibility.

—Charles F. Kettering

Laugh:
A smile that burst.

—John E. Donovan

I believe that any man's life will be filled with constant and unexpected encouragement if he makes up his mind to do his level best each day, and as nearly as possible reaches the high water mark of pure and useful living.

—Booker T. Washington

Hope is itself a species of happiness, and perhaps the chief happiness which this world affords.

—Samuel Johnson

JOY

The *unthankful heart*...discovers
no mercies; but let the thankful
heart sweep through the clay and,
as the magnet finds the iron, so
it will find, in every hour, some
heavenly blessings!

—Henry Ward Beecher

Grateful for the blessing
lent of simple tastes
and mind content!

—Oliver Wendell Holmes

For everything you have missed, you have gained something else.

—Ralph Waldo Emerson

Refrain from wanting what you have not, and cheerfully make the best of a bird in the hand.

—Seneca

Slight not what is near
through aiming at
what is far.

—Euripides

The greatest pleasure
I know, is to do a
good action by stealth,
and to have it found
out by accident.

—Charles Lamb

Gladly accept
the gifts of the
present hour.

—Horace

Nothing is worth
more than this day.

—Johann Wolfgang von Goethe

I could not, at any age, be content to take my place by the fireside and simply look on. Life was meant to be lived. Curiosity must be kept alive. One must never, for whatever reason, turn his back on life.

—Eleanor Roosevelt

If we live good lives, the

times are also good. As

we are,

such are

the times.

—Saint Augustine

JOY

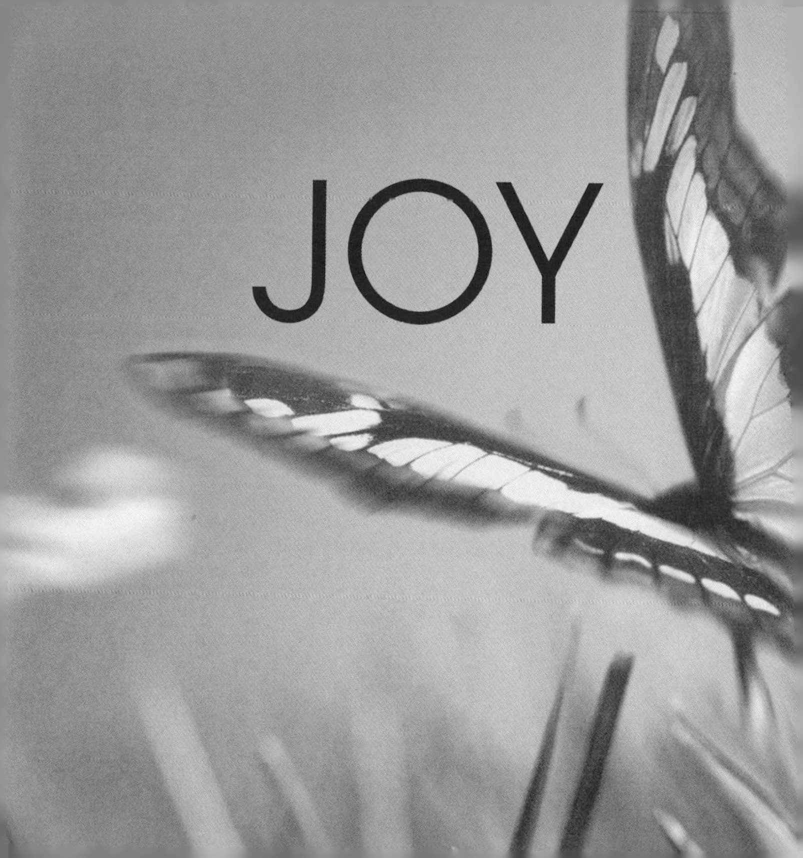

To love and be loved—

this on earth is the

highest bliss.

—Heinrich Heine

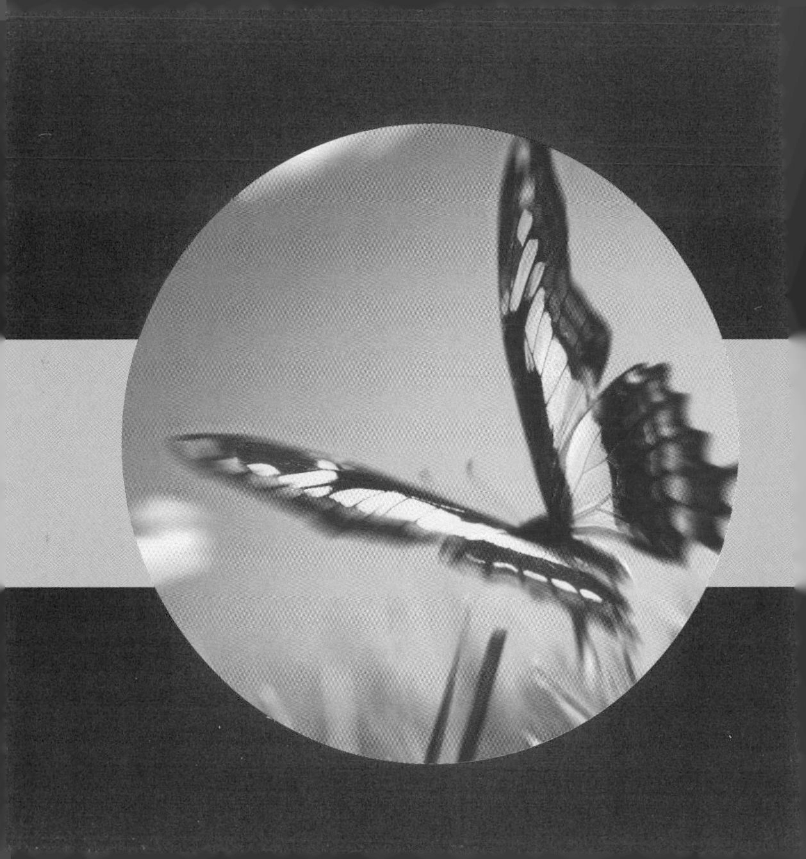

One should count each
day a separate life.

—Seneca

That man is
happiest who lives
from day to day
and asks no more,
garnering the simple
goodness of life.

—Euripides

We should consider *every day lost* on which we have not danced at least once.

—Friedrich Nietzsche

Our happiness
or unhappiness
depends as
much on our
temperaments
as on our luck.

—François de La
Rochefoucauld

To be without
some of the
things you
want is an
indispensable
part of
happiness.

—Bertrand Russell

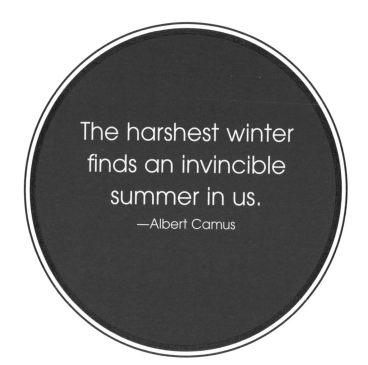

The harshest winter finds an invincible summer in us.
—Albert Camus

I find the great thing in

this world is not so much

where we stand as in what

direction we are moving.

—Oliver Wendell Holmes

I have known some quite good people who were unhappy, but never an interested person who was unhappy.

—A.C. Benson

JOY

Worry is a thin stream of fear trickling through the mind. If encouraged, it cuts a channel into which all other thoughts are drained.

—Arthur S. Roche

Free will, though it makes evil possible, is also the only thing that makes possible any

love of goodness

or joy worth having.

—C.S. Lewis

Go forth into
the busy world
and love it.
Interest yourself
in its life, mingle
kindly with its
joys and sorrows.

—Ralph Waldo Emerson

Day, with life and heart,
is more than time enough
to find a world.
—James Russell Lowell

This time, like all times, is a

very good one if we but

know what to do with it.

—Ralph Waldo Emerson

The man who makes
everything that leads
to happiness depend
upon himself, and not
upon other men, has
adopted the very best plan
for living happily.

—Plato

One today is worth
two tomorrows.

—Benjamin Franklin

The cares of today
are seldom those
of tomorrow.

—William Cowper

Do not look back
on happiness, or
dream of it in the
future. You are only
sure of today; do
not let yourself
be cheated
out of it.

—Henry Ward Beecher

Every second is of
infinite value.

—Johann Wolfgang von Goethe

JOY

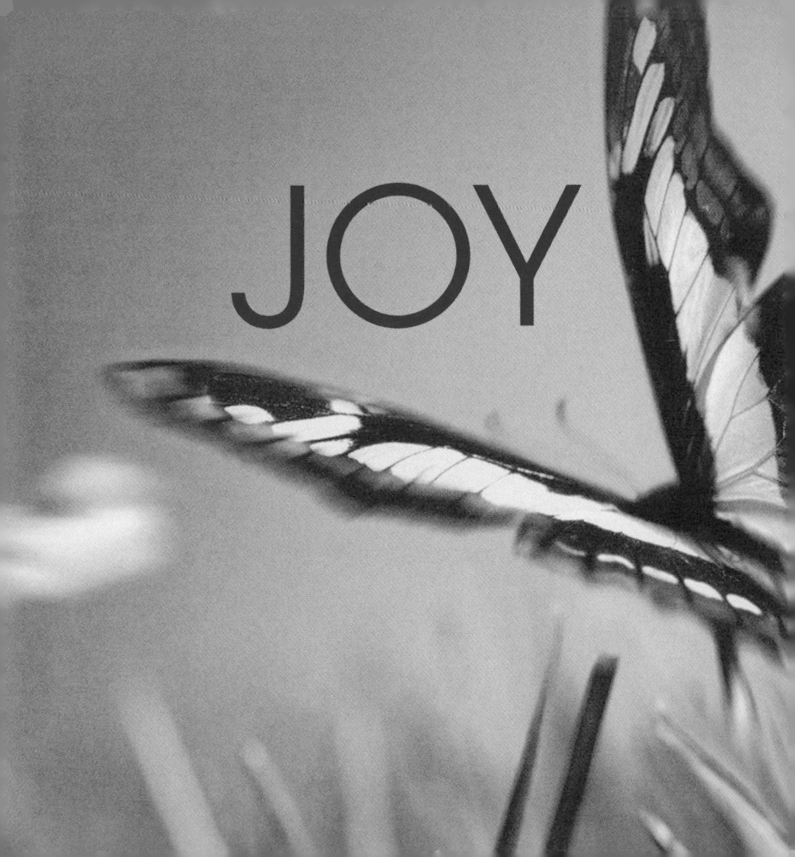

Let us then be up
and doing, with a heart
for any fate.

—Henry Wadsworth Longfellow

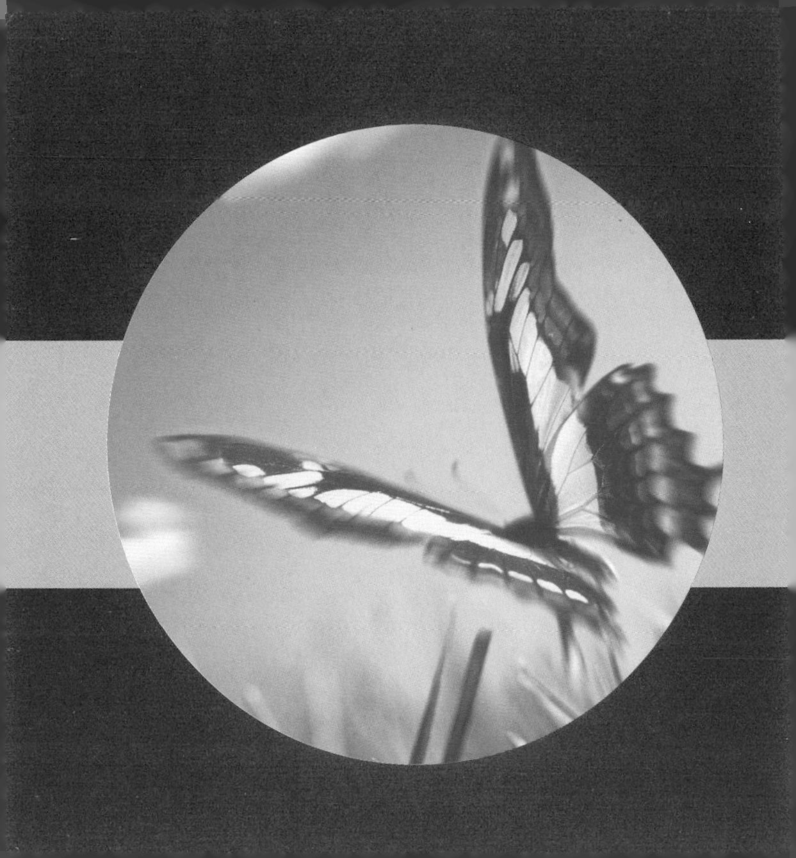

They who lose today
may win tomorrow.

—Miguel de Cervantes

Cease to inquire what the future has in store, and take as a gift whatever the day brings forth.

—Horace

So always look for

the *silver lining*

And try to find the

sunny side of life.

—P.G. Wodehouse

This, too,
shall pass.

—William Shakespeare

They can
because they
think they can.

—Virgil

If matters go badly
now, they will not
always be so.

—Horace

Dream lofty dreams,
and as you dream,
so shall you become.
Your vision is the
promise of what you
shall at last unveil.

—John Ruskin

Optimism is the faith that leads to achievement. Nothing can be done without hope and confidence.

—Helen Keller

JOY

There is in the worst of
fortune the best of
chances for a
happy change.

—Euripides

To keep our faces toward change,

and behave like free spirits in

the presence of fate, is

strength undefeatable.

—Helen Keller

Hope is the power of being cheerful in circumstances which we know to be desperate.

—G.K. Chesterton

We expect more of ourselves than we have any right to.

—Oliver Wendell Holmes Jr.

He who postpones the hour of living is like the rustic who waits for the river to run out before he crosses.

—Horace

Knowledge of what is

possible is the beginning

of happiness.

—George Santayana

He who has a *why* to
live for can bear
almost any *how*.

—Friedrich Nietzsche

Do the thing you
fear, and the death
of fear is certain.

—Ralph Waldo Emerson

We act as though comfort and luxury were the chief requirements of life, when all that we need to make us really happy is something to be enthusiastic about.

—Charles Kingsley

Happiness is excitement that has found a settling down place, but there is always a little corner that keeps flapping around.

—E.L. Konigsburg

JOY

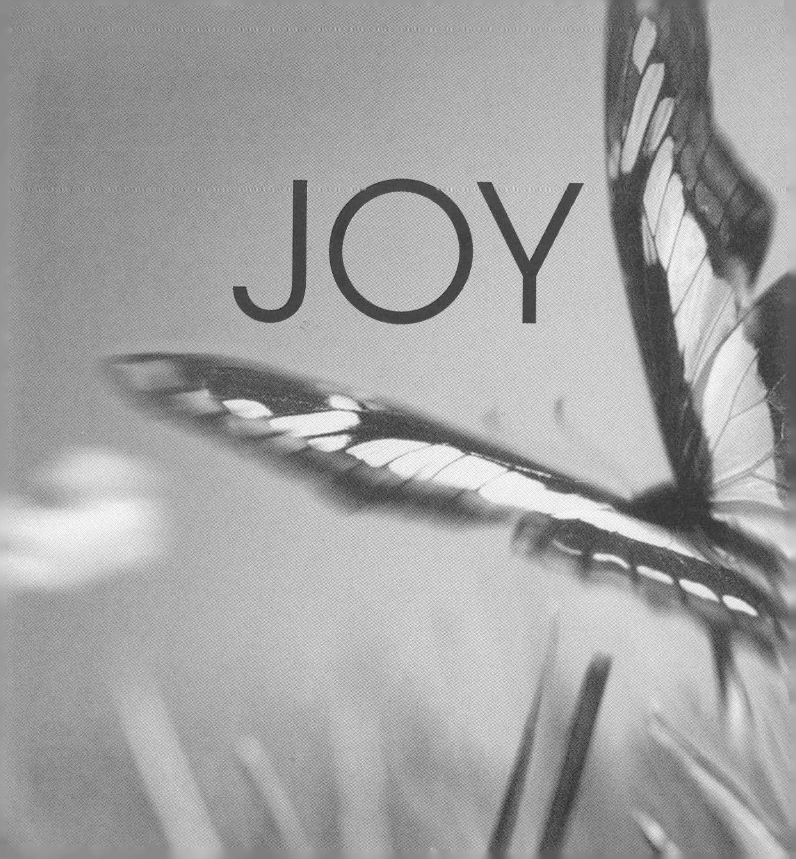

Joy rises in me,

like as a summer's morn.

—Samuel Taylor Coleridge

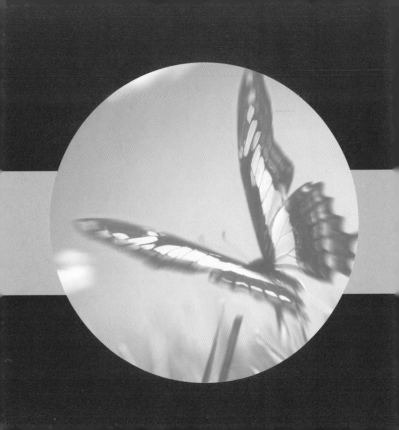

I steer my bark with
hope in my heart,
leaving fear astern.

—Thomas Jefferson

If all the griefs I am to have
Would only come today,
I am so happy I believe
They'd laugh and run away!

—Emily Dickinson

304

How much pain they have

cost us, the evils which

have never happened.

—Thomas Jefferson

That is but
a slippery
Happiness
which Fortune
can give and
can take away.

—Thomas Fuller

We are
very near to
greatness: one
step and we
are safe; can
we not take
the leap?

—Ralph Waldo Emerson

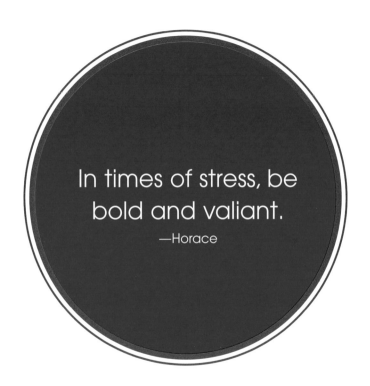

In times of stress, be bold and valiant.

—Horace

The first and indispensable

requisite of happiness is

a clear conscience.

—Edward Gibbon

What saves a *person*
is to take a step.
Then another step.

—Antoine de Saint-Exupéry

JOY

Luck is believing
you're lucky.

—Tennessee Williams

Precisely the least, the softest, lightest, a lizard's rustling, a breath, a breeze, a moment's glance—it is little that makes the best happiness.

—Friedrich Nietzsche

A good laugh

is sunshine in

a house.

—William Makepeace
Thackeray

Against the assault
of laughter nothing
can stand.

—Mark Twain

Happiness is not achieved by the conscious pursuit of happiness; it is generally the by-product of other activities.

—Aldous Huxley

Practice yourself in little things, and thence proceed to greater.

—Epictetus

If I accept sunshine
and warmth, then I
must also accept the
thunder and lightning.

—Kahlil Gibran

None but those
who are happy in
themselves can
make others so.

—William Hazlitt

My greatest
happiness
consists precisely
in doing nothing
whatever that
is calculated
to obtain
happiness.

—Chuang Tzu

Hope is like the *sun*,
which, as we journey
toward it, casts the
shadow
of our
burden
behind us.

—Samuel Smiles

JOY

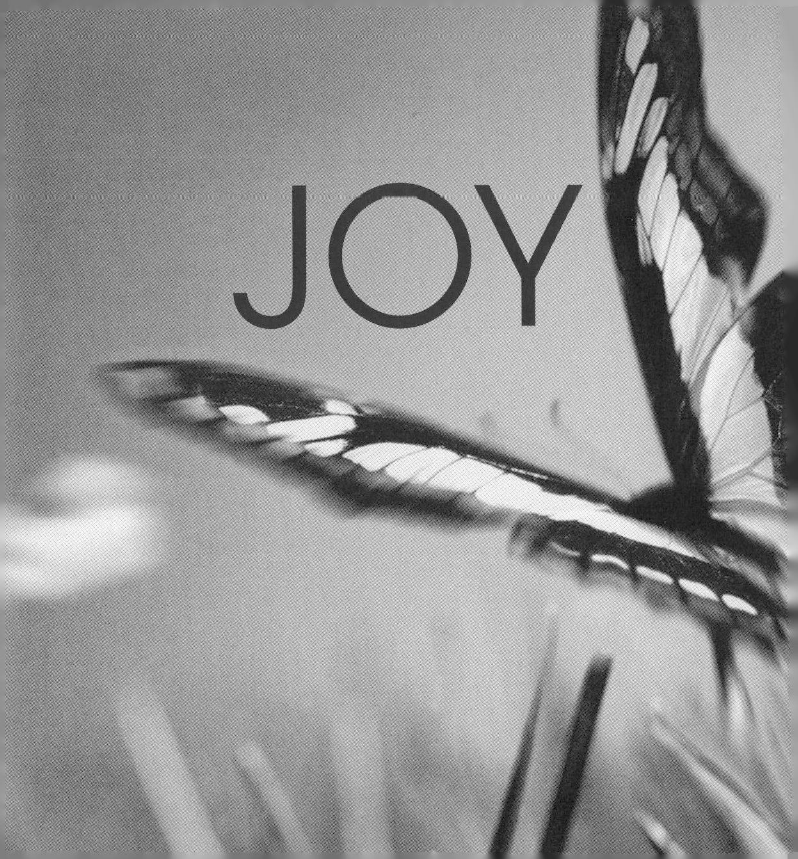

With the past,
I have nothing to do;
nor with the future.
I live now.

—Ralph Waldo Emerson

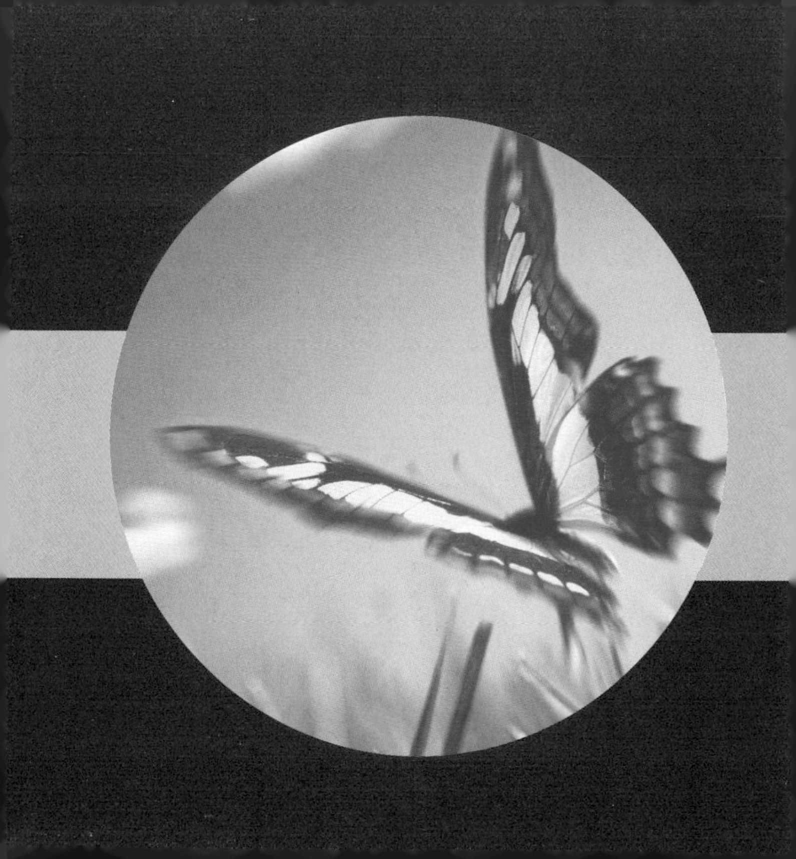

The strongest and sweetest songs yet remain to be sung.
—Walt Whitman

The bliss e'en of a moment still is bliss.

—Joanna Baillie

I expect to pass through this world but once; any good thing therefore that I can do, or any kindness that I can show to any fellow creature, let me do it now; let me not defer or neglect it, for I shall not pass this way again.

—Stephen Grellet

The mere sense
of living is joy
enough.

—Emily Dickinson

Content
is happiness.

—Thomas Fuller

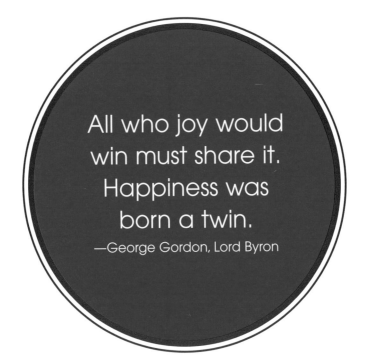

All who joy would win must share it. Happiness was born a twin.

—George Gordon, Lord Byron

The chief product of life
is really *JOY!*

JOY makes the

face shine and is

contentment that

fills the soul.

—Alfred A. Montapert

Who is rich?
He who rejoices
in his portion.

—Anonymous

JOY

Life is to be enjoyed,
to laugh, to sing, to
love, to meditate.

—Alfred A. Montapert

He who enjoys doing

and enjoys what he

has done is happy.

—Johann Wolfgang von Goethe

I love my past.
I love my present.
I'm not ashamed
of what I've had,
and I'm not sad
because I have
it no longer.

—Colette

Joy is the holy fire that keeps our purpose warm and our intelligence aglow.

—Helen Keller

Joy is a net of love

by which you

can catch souls.

—Mother Teresa

The more the heart is

sated with joy, the more it

becomes insatiable.

—Gabrielle Roy

Enthusiasm is
contagious.
Be a carrier.

—Susan Rabin

I cannot sleep –
great joy is as
restless as sorrow.

—Fanny Burney

Ecstasies inspire and awaken the soul; they convince the mind absolutely of the existence of another form of living.

—Anonymous

Birds sing after a storm; why shouldn't people feel as free to delight in whatever sunlight remains to them?

—Rose Kennedy

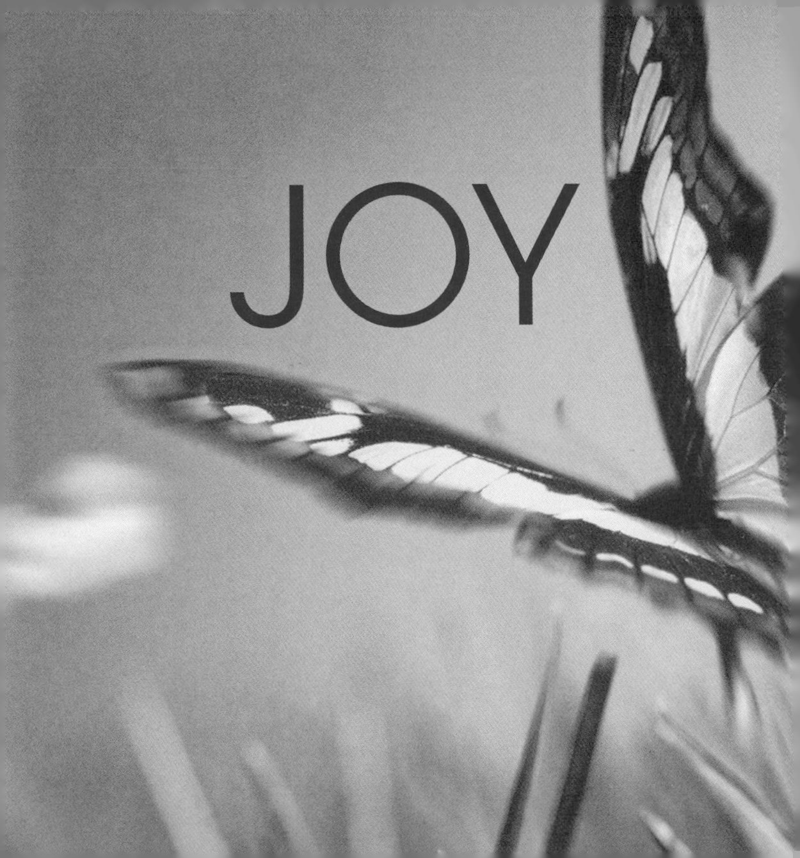
JOY

A good time

for laughing is

when you can.

—Jessamyn West

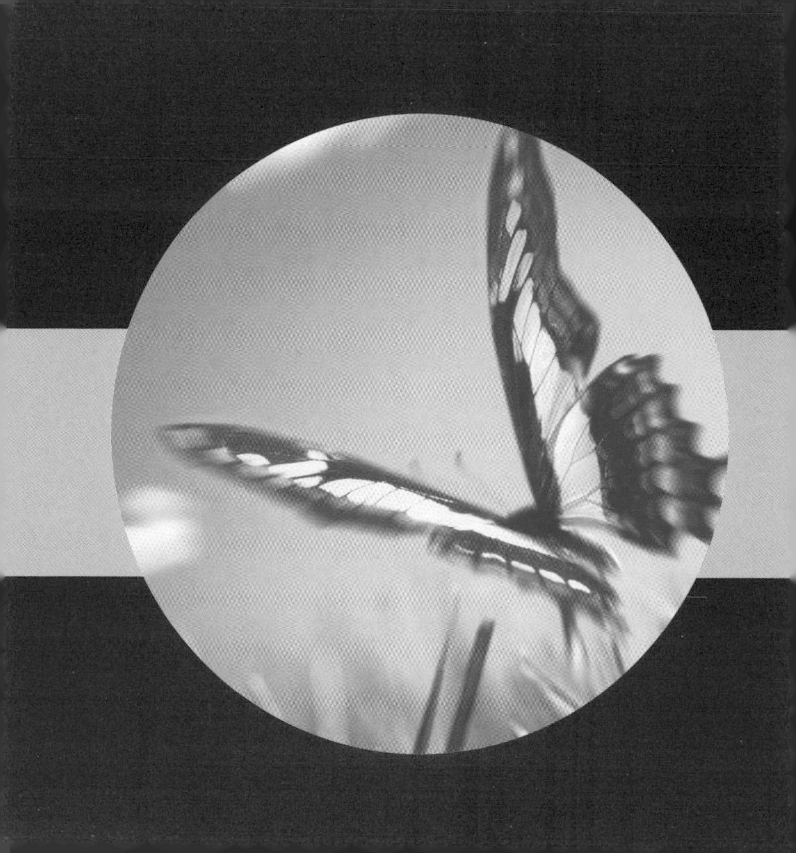

Laughter is by
definition healthy.

—Doris Lessing

Laughter is the lightning rod of play, the eroticism of conversation.

—Eva Hoffman

A garden isn't meant to be useful. It's for joy.

—Rumer Godden

Grab your coat, and
get your hat
Leave your worry on
the doorstep
Just direct your feet
To the sunny side of
the street.

—Dorothy Fields

If only men could
be induced to
laugh more they
might hate less, and
find more serenity
here on earth.

—Malcolm Muggeridge

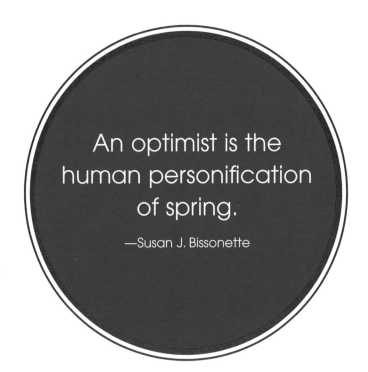

An optimist is the human personification of spring.

—Susan J. Bissonette

The game was to just find something about everything to be glad about—no matter what 'twas....You see, when you're hunting for the glad things, you sort of forget the other kind.

—Eleanor H. Porter

Worlds can be found by a child and an adult bending down and looking together under the grass stems or at the skittering crabs in a tidal pool.

—Mary Catherine Bateson

JOY

What feeling in all the world is so nice as that of a *child's hand in yours*? It is soft. It is small and warm. It is as *innocent* and *guileless* as a rabbit or a puppy or a kitten huddling in the shelter of your clasp.

—Marjorie Holmes

A happy woman is one
who has no cares at all;
a cheerful woman is one
who has cares but doesn't
let them get her down.

—Beverly Sills

Love and Joy
are twins,
or born of
each other.

—William Hazlitt

His laughter...
sparkled like a splash of
water in sunlight.

—Joseph Lelyveld

Thou dost show me

the path of life;

in thy presence there is

fullness of joy.

—Psalms 16:11

Winning is
important to me,
but what brings me real
joy is the experience of
being fully engaged in
whatever I'm doing.

—Phil Jackson

Happiness lies in the
absorption in some
vocation which
satisfies the soul.

—Sir William Osler

To live as fully, as
completely as possible,
to be happy, and again
to be happy is the true
aim and end of life.

—Llewelyn Powys

363

Mirth is like a flash of lightning, that breaks through a gloom of clouds, and glitters for a moment; *cheerfulness* keeps up a kind of daylight in the mind, and fills it with a steady and *perpetual serenity.*

—Joseph Addison

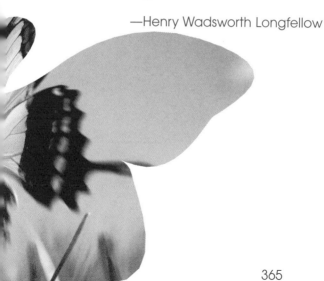

Enthusiasm

begets enthusiasm.

—Henry Wadsworth Longfellow

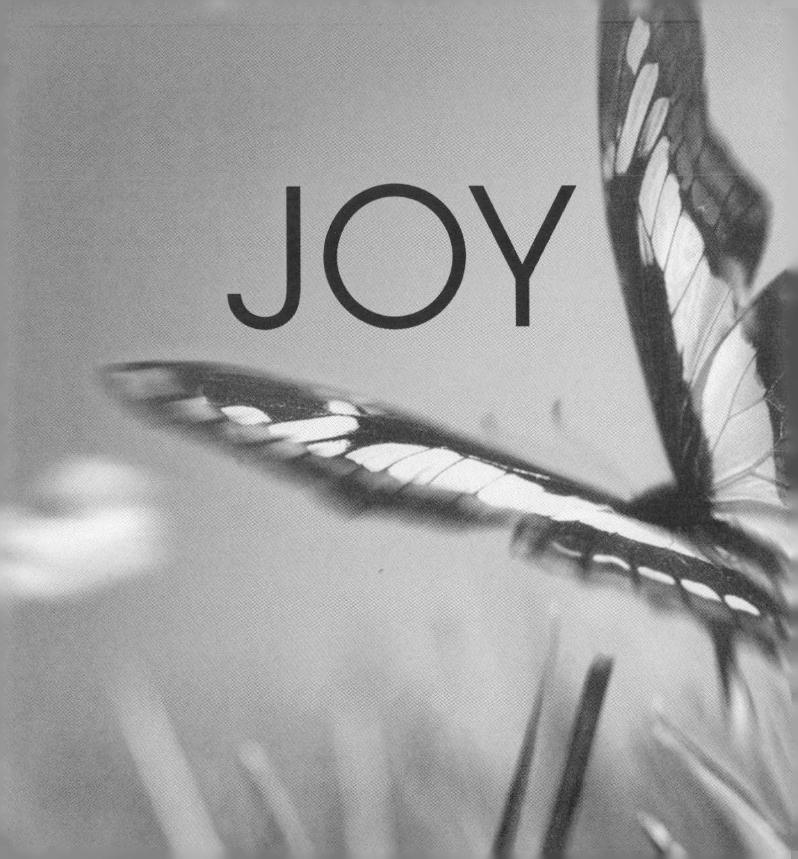
JOY

There'll be bluebirds
over the white cliffs of
Dover, tomorrow,
just you wait and see.

—Nat Burton

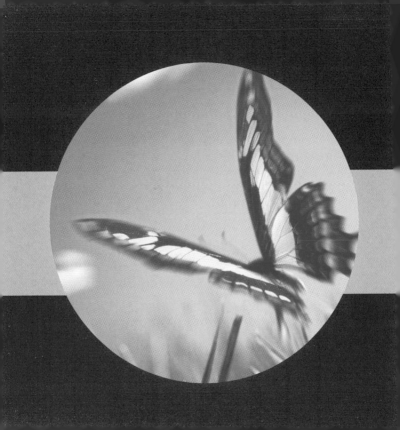

We have to laugh. Because laughter, we already know, is the first evidence of freedom.

—Rosario Castellanos

It is so much easier to be enthusiastic than to reason!

—Eleanor Roosevelt

Inebriate of Air—am I—
And Debauchee of Dew—
Reeling—through endless
summer days—
From inns of Molten Blue—

—Emily Dickinson

A little
Madness in
the Spring
Is wholesome
even for
the King.

—Emily Dickinson

He that is of
a merry
heart hath a
continual feast.

—Proverbs 15:15

Make a joyful noise unto the Lord, all ye lands. Serve the Lord with gladness: come before his presence with singing.

—Psalm 100:1,2

Weeping may endure for a night, but joy cometh in the morning.

—Psalm 30:5

This is the day which the
Lord hath made. Let us
rejoice and be glad in it.

—Psalm 118:24,25

JOY

A merry *heart* doeth
good like a medicine.

—Psalm 17:22

That's joy, it's always

a recognition, the known

appearing fully itself, and

more itself than one knew.

—Denise Levertov

Love to faults is
always blind,
Always is to joy
inclined,
Lawless, winged,
and unconfined,
And breaks all chains
from every mind.

—William Blake